ollins

C000178305

SNAP
REVISION

ELEMENTS, COMPOUNDS AND MIXTURES & CHEMICAL REACTIONS

OCR Gateway GCSE Chemistry

OCR
GATEWAY
GCSE
CHEMISTRY

REVISE TRICKY
TOPICS IN A SNAP

Contents

Published by Collins
An imprint of HarperCollinsPublishers
1 London Bridge Street,
London, SE1 9GF

© HarperCollinsPublishers Limited 2016

9780008218126

First published 2016

10 9 8 7 6 5 4 3 2 1

ACKNOWLEDGEMENTS

The author and publisher are grateful to the copyright holders for permission to use quoted materials and images.

Every effort has been made to trace copyright holders and obtain their permission for the use of copyright material. The author and publisher will gladly receive information enabling them to rectify any error or omission in subsequent editions. All facts are correct at time of going to press.

HT Higher Tier content

How To Use This Book

To get the most out of this revision guide, just work your way through the book in the order it is presented.

This is how it works:

Revise
Clear and concise revision notes help you get to grips with the topic

Revise
Key Points and Key Words explain the important information you need to know

Revise
A Quick Test at the end of every topic is a great way to check your understanding

Practise
Practice questions for each topic reinforce the revision content you have covered

Review
The Review section is a chance to revisit the topic to improve your recall in the exam

Purity and Separating Mixtures

You must be able to:

- Suggest appropriate methods to separate substances
- Work out empirical formulae using relative molecular masses and relative formula masses
- Calculate the R$_f$ values of different substances that have been separated using chromatography.

Purity

- In chemistry something is pure if all of the particles that make up that substance are the same, e.g. pure gold only contains gold atoms and pure water only contains water molecules.
- All substances have a specific melting point at room temperature and pressure.
- Comparing the actual melting point to this known value is a way of checking the purity of a substance.
- Any impurities cause the substance to melt at a different temperature.
- **Formulations** are mixtures that have been carefully designed to have specific properties, e.g. alloys.

Key Point

In the world outside the lab, 'pure' is often used to describe mixtures, e.g. milk. This means that nothing has been added; it does not indicate how *chemically* pure it is.

Relative Atomic, Formula and Molecular Mass

- Every element has its own relative atomic mass (A$_r$).
- This is the ratio of the average mass of one atom of the element to one-twelfth of the mass of an atom of carbon-12.
- The relative molecular mass (M$_r$) is the sum of the relative atomic masses of each atom making up a molecule.
- For example, the M$_r$ of O$_2$ is $2 \times 16 = 32$.
- The relative formula mass (M$_r$) is the sum of the relative atomic masses of all the atoms that make up a compound.

For example, the relative atomic mass of magnesium is 24 and of oxygen is 16.

Calculate the relative formula mass of H$_2$O.

H:	$2 \times 1 = 2$
O:	$1 \times 16 = 16$
H$_2$O:	$2 + 16 = 18$

Multiply the number of atoms of each element in the molecule by the relative atomic mass.

Add them all up to calculate the M$_r$.

Empirical Formula

- The empirical formula is the simplest whole number ratio of each type of atom in a compound.
- It can be calculated from the numbers of atoms present or by converting the mass of the element or compound.

Key Point

Always show your working-out when calculating empirical formulae. You will be less likely to make mistakes if you do.

What is the empirical formula of a compound with the formula C$_6$H$_{12}$O$_6$?

$$C = \frac{6}{6} = 1 \qquad H = \frac{12}{6} = 2 \qquad O = \frac{6}{6} = 1$$

The empirical formula is written as CH$_2$O.

Work out the smallest ratio of whole numbers by dividing each by the smallest number. This would be C$_1$H$_2$O$_1$.

Remember, the 1 is not written.

- For example, all alkenes have the empirical formula C_1H_2 although the 1 is not written, so it would be appear as CH_2.

What is the empirical formula of a compound containing 24g of carbon, 8g of hydrogen and 32g of oxygen?

Elements	Carbon	:	Hydrogen	:	Oxygen
Mass of element	24	:	8	:	32
A_r of element	12	:	1	:	16
$\dfrac{\text{Mass of element}}{A_r}$	2	:	8	:	2
Divide by smallest number	÷ 2		÷ 2		÷ 2
Ratio of atoms in empirical formula	1	:	4	:	1

The empirical formula is therefore CH_4O.

List all the elements in the compound.

To find the number of moles, divide the mass of each element by its relative atomic mass.

Divide each answer by the smallest number in step 2 to obtain a ratio.

The ratio may have to be scaled up to give whole numbers.

Remember, it is incorrect to write the 1 for an element.

Separation Techniques

- Techniques that can be used to separate mixtures include:
- **Filtration** – a solid is separated from a liquid (e.g. copper oxide solid in copper sulfate solution).
- **Crystallisation** – a solvent is evaporated off to leave behind a solute in crystal form (e.g. salt in water).
- **Distillation** – two liquids with significantly different boiling points are separated, i.e. when heated, the liquid with the lowest boiling point evaporates first and the vapour is condensed and collected.
- **Fractional distillation** – a mixture of liquids with different boiling points are separated (e.g. petrol from crude oil).
- Chromatography – substances in a mixture are separated using a stationary phase and a mobile phase.
  - **Paper chromatography** – this is useful for separating mixtures of dyes in solution (e.g. dyes in ink).
  - **Thin layer chromatography (TLC)** – this is more accurate than paper chromatography and uses a thin layer of an inert solid for the stationary phase.
  - **Gas chromatography** – this separates gas mixtures by passing them through a solid stationary phase.
- Substances separated by chromatography can be identified by calculating their R_f values.

$$R_f = \frac{\text{distance moved by the compound}}{\text{distance moved by the solvent}}$$

- Separated substances can be identified by comparing the results to known R_f values.

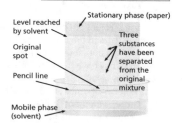

Level reached by solvent

Original spot

Pencil line

Stationary phase (paper)

Three substances have been separated from the original mixture

Mobile phase (solvent)

Key Words

formulations
relative atomic mass (A_r)
relative molecular mass (M_r)
relative formula mass (M_r)
chromatography
stationary phase
mobile phase
R_f value

Quick Test

1. What is the relative formula mass of $Mg(OH)_2$?
2. What is paper chromatography used to separate?
3. What is the empirical formula of a compound with the formula C_2H_6?

Bonding

You must be able to:

- Explain how metals and non-metals are positioned in the periodic table
- Describe the electronic structure of an atom
- Draw dot and cross diagrams for ions and simple covalent molecules.

The Periodic Table

- An element contains one type of atom.
- Elements cannot be chemically broken down into simpler substances.
- There are about 100 naturally occurring elements.
- The design of the modern periodic table was first developed by Mendeleev.
- Elements in Mendeleev's table were placed into groups based on their atomic mass.
- Mendeleev's method was testable and predicted elements not yet discovered.
- However, some elements were put in the wrong place because the values used for their atomic masses were incorrect.
- The modern periodic table is a modified version of Mendeleev's table.
- It takes into account the arrangement of electrons, the number of electrons in the outermost shell, and atomic number.

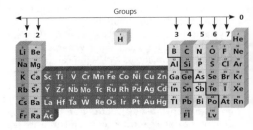

Groups

- A vertical column of elements in the periodic table is a group.
- Lithium (Li), sodium (Na) and potassium (K) are in Group 1.
- Elements in the same group have similar chemical properties because they have the same number of electrons in their outer shell (or energy level).
- The number of outer electrons is the same as the group number:
  - Group 1 elements have one electron in their outer shell.
  - Group 7 elements have seven electrons in their outer shell.
  - Group 0 elements have a full outer shell.

Periods

- A horizontal row of elements in the periodic table is a period.
- Lithium (Li), carbon (C) and neon (Ne) are in Period 2.
- The period for an element is related to the number of occupied electron shells it has.
- For example, sodium (Na), aluminium (Al) and chlorine (Cl) have three shells of electrons so they are in Period 3.

> **Key Point**
>
> The number of protons in a nucleus of an element never changes. That's why the periodic table shows the atomic number.

Metals and Non-Metals

- The majority of the elements in the periodic table are metals.
- Metals are very useful materials because of their properties:
  - They are lustrous, e.g. gold is used in jewellery.
  - They are hard and have a high density, e.g. titanium is used to make steel for drill parts.
  - They have high tensile strength (are able to bear loads), e.g. steel is used to make bridge girders.
  - They have high melting and boiling points, e.g. tungsten is used to make light-bulb filaments.
  - They are good conductors of heat and electricity, e.g. copper is used to make pans and wiring.
- Metals can react with non-metals to form ionic compounds.
- For example, metals react with oxygen to form metal oxides.

Electronic Structure

- An element's position in the periodic table can be worked out from its electronic structure.
- For example, sodium's electronic structure is 2.8.1 (atomic number = 11):
  - It has three orbital shells, so it can be found in Period 3.
  - It has one electron in its outer shell, so it can be found in Group 1.
- The electronic structure can also be shown using a dot and cross diagram, in which each cross represents an electron.

Chemical Bonds

- Chemical bonds are *not* physical structures.
- They are the transfer or sharing of electrons, which leads to the atoms involved becoming more stable.
- An ionic bond is formed when one or more electrons are donated by one atom or molecule and received by another atom or molecule.
- When an ionic compound is in solution, or in a molten state, the ions move freely.
- When an ionic compound is solid, ions are arranged in a way to cancel out the charges.
- A covalent bond is formed when atoms share electrons to complete their outermost shell.

Sodium atom, Na
2.8.1

Sodium ion, Na$^+$
[2.8]$^+$

+ 1e$^-$

● Positively charged ion ● Negatively charged ion

Quick Test

1. Give two ways that elements are arranged in the modern periodic table.
2. Draw a dot and cross diagram to show the electronic structure of magnesium.
3. Write the electronic structure for chlorine.

Models of Bonding

You must be able to:

- Describe and compare the type of bonds in different substances and their arrangement
- Use a variety of models to represent molecules
- Identify the limitations of different models.

Models of Bonding

- **Models** can be used to show how atoms are bonded together.
- Dot and cross diagrams can show:
  - each shell of electrons or just the outer shell
  - how electrons are donated or shared.
- Methane is a **covalent** compound. Each molecule is made up of a carbon atom joined to four hydrogens (CH_4).

Methane, CH_4

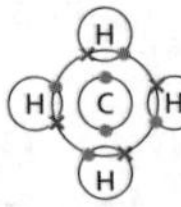

Methane, CH_4

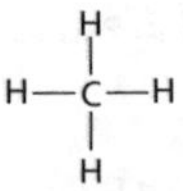

> Each line or shared pair of electrons shows a covalent bond.

Methane, CH_4

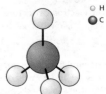

- Ball and stick models give an idea of the 3D shape of a molecule or compound.
- Each model has limitations:
  - The scale of the nucleus to the electrons is wrong in most models.
  - Models show bonds as physical structures.
  - Most models do not give an accurate idea of the 3D shape of a molecule.
  - The bond lengths are not in proportion to the size of the atoms.
  - Models aid our understanding about molecules, but they are not the real thing.

Ion Formation

- Metals give away electrons to become positive ions:

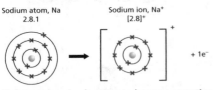

Sodium atom, Na
2.8.1

Sodium ion, Na⁺
[2.8]⁺

+ 1e⁻

- Non-metals gain electrons to become negative ions:

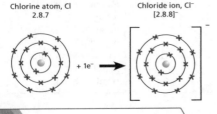

Chlorine atom, Cl
2.8.7

+ 1e⁻

Chloride ion, Cl⁻
[2.8.8]⁻

Key Point

Scientists use models to help solve problems. As atoms are too small to be seen with the naked eye, models are a helpful way of visualising them.

> Sodium gives away a single electron to become a Na⁺ ion.

> Chlorine gains an electron to become a Cl⁻ ion.

- Ionic bonds are the electrostatic forces of attraction that hold the ions together.

Simple Molecules

- When non-metals or non-ionic molecules join together, the atoms share electrons and form a covalent bond. These are called simple molecules.
- Hydrogen gas, H_2, is a covalent molecule.

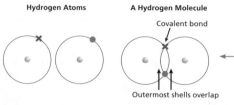

Hydrogen Atoms   A Hydrogen Molecule

Covalent bond

Outermost shells overlap

Key Point

The term 'ionic bond' suggests there is a permanent, physical link between ions. However, when in solution or molten, the ions move further away from each other.

Each hydrogen atom now has a full outermost shell, with two electrons.

Giant Covalent Structures

- Giant covalent structures are formed when the atoms of a substance form repeated covalent bonds.
- Silicon dioxide is a compound made up of repeating silicon and oxygen atoms joined by single covalent bonds.

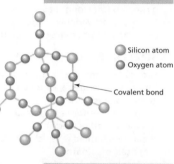

Silicon atom

Oxygen atom

Covalent bond

Polymers

- A polymer is formed when repeated units are covalently bonded together.
- For example, when lots of ethene molecules are joined together they form poly(ethene).

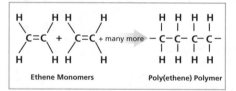

Ethene Monomers   Poly(ethene) Polymer

Atoms are shown by their element symbol. Bonds are shown with lines. Two lines together indicate a double bond (two covalent bonds between atoms).

Metals

- Metal atoms are held together by strong metallic bonds.
- The metal atoms lose their outermost electrons and become positively charged.
- The electrons can move freely from one metal ion to another.
- This causes a sea of delocalised (free) electrons to be formed.

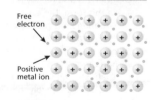

Free electron

Positive metal ion

Key Words

model
covalent
ionic bond
simple molecule
giant covalent structure
polymer
delocalised

Quick Test

1. What is meant by the term 'sea of delocalised electrons'?
2. Give two limitations of a dot and cross model of a covalent compound.
3. What is meant by the term 'giant covalent structure'?

Properties of Materials

You must be able to:

- Describe how carbon can form a wide variety of different molecules
- Explain the properties of diamond, graphite, fullerenes and graphene
- Explain what nanoparticles are and the risks they pose.

Carbon

- Carbon is the sixth element in the periodic table and has an atomic mass of 12.
- Carbon is in Group 4 because it has four electrons in its outer shell.
- This means that it can make up to four covalent bonds with other atoms.
- It can also form long chains of atoms and rings.
- There is a vast variety of naturally occurring and synthetic (man-made) carbon-based compounds, called organic compounds.

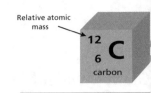

Relative atomic mass

12
6 **C**
carbon

Allotropes of Carbon

- Each carbon atom can bond with up to four other carbon atoms.
- Different structures are formed depending on how many carbon atoms bond together.
- These different forms are called allotropes of carbon. They do not contain any other elements.
- Graphite is formed when each carbon atom bonds with three other carbon atoms:
  - Graphite has free electrons so it can conduct electricity, e.g. in electrolysis.
  - The layers are held together by weak bonds, so they can break off easily, e.g. in drawing pencils and as a dry lubricant.
- Graphene is a single layer of graphite:
  - In this form, the carbon is 207 times stronger than steel.
  - Graphene has free electrons so it can conduct electricity.
  - It is used in electronics and solar panels.
- Diamond is formed when each carbon atom bonds with four other carbon atoms:
  - Diamond cannot conduct electricity, as all its outermost electrons are involved in bonding.
  - Diamonds are very hard. They are used in drill bits and polished diamonds are used in jewellery.
  - Diamond is extremely strong because each atom forms the full number of covalent bonds.

> **Key Point**
>
> There are a few carbon compounds that are non-organic. They include the oxides of carbon, cyanides, carbonates and carbides.

Graphite

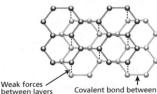

Weak forces between layers

Covalent bond between two carbon atoms within a layer

Graphene

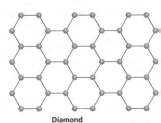

Diamond

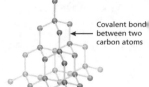

Covalent bond between two carbon atoms

- **Fullerenes** are tubes and spherical structures formed using only carbon atoms:
  - They are used as superconductors, for reinforcing carbon-fibre structures, and as containers for drugs being introduced into the body.

Structure of
Buckminsterfullerene

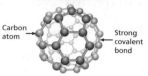

Carbon atom → (Strong covalent bond)

Bonding and Changing State

- Bonding is an attraction between atoms in elements and compounds.
- If the attraction is weak, then it is easy to separate the atoms compared to those with a stronger attraction.
- The ions in ionic substances are more easily separated when they are in solution or molten, as they can move about freely.
- When an ionic substance is in its crystal (solid) form, i.e. when the distance between ions is at its smallest, it is very difficult to separate the ions due to the strong electrostatic forces.
- They form a giant lattice structure.
- The melting point of ionic substances is, therefore, very high.
- For example, the melting point of NaCl is 801°C.
- Covalent bonds are very strong.
- If there are a lot of bonds, e.g. in a giant covalent compound, the melting point will be very high (higher than for ionic compounds).
- For example, graphite melts at 3600°C.
- Simple covalent molecules have very low boiling points.
- The simplest gas, hydrogen, melts at −259°C and has a boiling point of −252.87°C.
- This is because the intermolecular forces that hold all the molecules together are weak and, therefore, easily broken.

Nanoparticles

- Nanoparticles are particles with a size between 1 and 100nm.
- Hydrogen atoms, by comparison are 0.1nm wide.
- At this size range all materials lose their bulk properties.
- For example, copper is bendy above 50nm, but nanoparticles of copper are ultra-strong and cannot be bent.
- Using nanoparticle materials opens up a new range of properties.
- For this reason, they are increasingly being used in a wide variety of industries, from medicine to construction.
- Nanoparticles exist naturally and can also be manufactured.
- They are small enough to enter respiratory systems and could potentially cause damage.
- They have a very high surface area compared to their volume, so they can act as catalysts.
- Silver nanoparticles can kill bacteria, both good and bad. The effect on the immune system is not known.

Key Point

Don't confuse intermolecular forces (the forces between molecules) with the intramolecular forces (e.g. the covalent bonds between the atoms in the molecules).

Key Point

There are 1 million nm per mm, 10 million nm per cm and 1 billion nm per m.

Key Point

It is important that scientists consider the risks and benefits of new technologies before introducing them to the outside world.

Key Words

organic
allotropes
graphene
fullerenes
intermolecular force
nanoparticle
bulk properties

Quick Test

1. What is meant by the term 'organic compound'?
2. Why is diamond so strong?
3. What is the size range for a nanoparticle?

Practice Questions

Purity and Separating Mixtures

1 **a)** What does the term **pure** mean in chemistry? [1]

b) Describe how melting points can be used to help identify a pure substance. [2]

2 Athina is separating food colourings using chromatography.

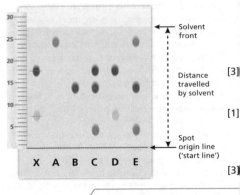

a) Calculate the R$_f$ value for the two colours in **X**. Show your working. [3]

b) Which of the food colourings, **A, B, C, D** or **E**, matches **X**? [1]

3 What is the empirical formula of a compound containing 84g of carbon, 16g of hydrogen and 64g of oxygen? Show your working. [3]

Total Marks _____ / 10

Bonding

1 Look at the following chemical symbols from the periodic table.

a) Write down the atomic number for each element. [2]

1 **H** hydrogen 1.0	11 **Na** sodium 23.0	12 **Mg** magnesium 24.3	6 **C** carbon 12.0
8 **O** oxygen 16.0	19 **K** potassium 39.1	20 **Ca** calcium 40.1	13 **Al** aluminum 27.0

b) Potassium oxide has the formula: K$_2$O.
Work out the **relative formula mass** for K$_2$O. [1]

c) Calculate the **relative molecular mass** for oxygen. [1]

2 The electronic structure of potassium, K, is written as 2.8.8.1.

a) Which of the following dot and cross diagrams represents K?

A   B   C   D   E   F

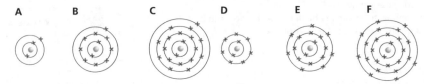

[1]

b) Write down the electronic structures for **B** and **E**. [2]

c) What do the **X** symbols represent in the diagrams? [1]

Total Marks _____ / 8

Models of Bonding

1. a) Describe what is meant by the term **ion**. [1]

    b) Draw the dot and cross diagram for a sodium ion, Na^+, and a chloride ion, Cl^-. [2]

2. a) Describe what is meant by the term **covalent bond**. [2]

    b) Chlorine gas, Cl_2, is a covalent molecule.

    Use a dot and cross diagram to show the covalent bond between the chlorine atoms. [2]

    Total Marks _____ / 7

Properties of Materials

1. a) Explain how carbon can form a variety of different molecules. [3]

    b) Describe what is meant by the term **allotrope**. [1]

    c) Give the names of **three** allotropes of carbon. [3]

2. Graphene is used in electronics and solar panels.

    Graphene

    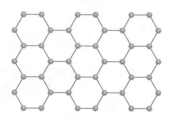

    a) Explain why graphene is used for these purposes. [2]

    b) Other than cost, explain why diamond is **not** used for these purposes. [1]

    c) Draw the structure of diamond. [2]

3. Ionic compounds can conduct electricity.

    a) Describe the conditions required for an ionic compound to conduct electricity. [2]

    b) Why do ionic compounds in their crystalline form typically have very high melting points? [2]

    Total Marks _____ / 16

Introducing Chemical Reactions

You must be able to:

- Use names and symbols to write formulae and balanced chemical equations
- Describe the states of reactants and products in a chemical reaction.

Law of Conservation of Mass

- The law of conservation of mass means that no atoms are created or destroyed.
- This means that, in a chemical reaction, the mass of the **products** will always equal the mass of the **reactants**.
- The atoms in a reaction can recombine with other atoms, but there will be no change in the overall number of atoms.
- This allows chemists to make predictions about chemical reactions. For example:
  - What might be formed when chemicals react together?
  - How much of the chemical or chemicals will be made?

Key Point

Chemicals are not 'used up' in a reaction. The atoms are rearranged into different chemicals.

Formulae and State Symbols

- Compounds can be represented using **formulae**, which use symbols and numbers to show:
  - the different elements in the compound
  - the number of atoms of each element in a molecule of the compound.
- A small subscript number following a symbol is a multiplier – it tells you how many of those atoms are present in a molecule.
- If there are brackets around part of the formula, everything inside the brackets is multiplied by the number on the outside.

Sulfuric acid has the formula H_2SO_4.
This means that there are two hydrogen atoms, one sulfur atom and four oxygen atoms.

The ratio of the number of atoms of each element in sulfuric acid is 2H : 1S : 4O.

$Ca(NO_3)_2$
This means that there is one calcium atom and two nitrate (NO_3) groups.
In total there are one calcium, two nitrogen and six oxygen atoms present in this compound.

- There are four state symbols, which are written in brackets after the formula symbols and numbers:
  - (s) = solid
  - (l) = liquid
  - (g) = gas
  - (aq) = aqueous (dissolved in water).

$H_2O(l)$ $CO_2(g)$ $H_2SO_4(aq)$ $S_8(s)$

Balancing Equations

- Equations show what happens during a chemical reaction.
- The reactants are on the left-hand side of the equation and the products are on the right.
- Remember, no atoms are lost or gained during a chemical reaction so the equation must be balanced.
- There must always be the same number of each type of atom on both sides of the equation.
- A large number written before a molecule is a coefficient – it is a multiplier that tells you how many copies of that whole molecule there are.

$2H_2SO_4$(aq) means there are two molecules of H_2SO_4(aq) present.

- To balance an equation:

Reactants			→	Products
magnesium	+	oxygen	→	magnesium oxide
Mg	+	O_2	→	MgO

Write the word equation.

Write the formulae of the reactants and products.

Balance the equation.

Add state symbols.

2Mg(s)	+	O_2(g)	→	2MgO(s)

- You should be able to balance equations by looking at the formulae without drawing the atoms. For example:

calcium carbonate	+	nitric acid	→	calcium nitrate	+	carbon dioxide	+	water
$CaCO_3$	+	HNO_3	→	$Ca(NO_3)_2$	+	CO_2	+	H_2O
$CaCO_3$	+	$2HNO_3$	→	$Ca(NO_3)_2$	+	CO_2	+	H_2O
$CaCO_3$(s)	+	$2HNO_3$(aq)	→	$Ca(NO_3)_2$(aq)	+	CO_2(g)	+	H_2O(l)

- Equations can also be written using displayed formulae. These must be balanced too.

Key Point

If you find the numbers keep on increasing on both sides of an equation you are trying to balance, it is likely you have made a mistake. Restart by checking the formulae and then rebalancing the equation.

Key Words

products
reactants
formulae
solid
liquid
gas
aqueous
coefficient

Quick Test

1. What is the formula of calcium hydroxide?
2. Write the balanced symbol equation for the reaction: sodium + chlorine → sodium chloride.
3. How many of each atom are present in this formula: $2MgSO_4$?

Chemical Equations

You must be able to:

- Recall the formulae of common ions and use them to deduce the formula of a compound
- HT Use names and symbols to write balanced half equations
- HT Construct balanced ionic equations.

Formulae of Common Ions

- Positive ions are called cations. Negative ions are called anions.
- There are a number of common ions that have a set charge.
- The roman numerals after a transition metal's name tell you its charge, e.g. iron(II) will have the charge Fe^{2+}.
- When combining ions to make an ionic compound, it is important that the charges cancel each other out so the overall charge is neutral.

> $Cu^{2+} + Cl^-$ ◄
> The formula is: $CuCl_2$

> **Key Point**
>
> Although ionic compounds are written as a formula (e.g. $CuCl_2$), they are actually dissociated when in solution, i.e. the ions separate from each other.

Two negative charges are needed to cancel the charge on the copper cation. These will come from having two chloride ions.

HT Stoichiometry

- Stoichiometry is the measurement of the relative amounts of reactants and products in chemical reactions.
- It is based on the conservation of mass, so knowing quantities or masses on one side of an equation enables you to work out the quantities or masses on the other side of the equation.

- For example, when magnesium is heated in air:
  $2Mg(s) + O_2(g) \rightarrow 2MgO(s)$
  - The mass of magnesium oxide formed is equal to the starting mass of magnesium plus the mass of oxygen from the air that is added to it.
- For example, when calcium carbonate is heated in air it thermally decomposes to form calcium oxide and carbon dioxide:
  $CaCO_3(s) \rightarrow CaO(s) + CO_2(g)$
  - The mass of calcium oxide remaining plus the mass of carbon dioxide added to the atmosphere is equal to the starting mass of calcium carbonate.

HT When looking at the stoichiometry of a chemical reaction it is common to look at the ratios of the molecules and compounds to each other.

- The numbers needed to balance an equation can be calculated from the masses of the reactants and the products using moles.

> In a chemical reaction, 72g of magnesium was reacted with exactly 48g of oxygen molecules to produce 120g of magnesium oxide.
>
> Use the number of moles of reactants and products to write a balanced equation for the reaction.

$$\text{amount of Mg} = \frac{72}{24} = 3\text{mol}$$

$$\text{amount of O}_2 = \frac{48}{32} = 1.5\text{mol}$$

$$\text{amount of MgO} = \frac{120}{40} = 3\text{mol}$$

$$3Mg + 1.5O_2 \rightarrow 3MgO$$

$$2Mg + O_2 \rightarrow 2MgO$$

> Use the masses of the reactants to calculate the number of moles present.

> Divide the number of moles of each substance by the smallest number (1.5) to give the simplest whole number ratio.

> This shows that 2 moles of magnesium react with 1 mole of oxygen molecules to produce 2 moles of magnesium oxide.

Limiting Reactants

* Sometimes when two chemicals react together, one chemical is completely used up during the reaction.
* When one chemical is used up, it stops the reaction going any further. It is called the limiting reactant.
* The other chemical, which is not used up, is said to be in excess.

Hydrogen ions to hydrogen gas:
1. Write formulae: $H^+ \rightarrow H_2$
2. Balance numbers: $2H^+ \rightarrow H_2$
3. Identify charges: 2^+ 0
4. Add electrons: $2H^+ + 2e^- \rightarrow H_2$

HT Half Equations

* Half equations can be written to show the changes that occur to the individual ions in a reaction:
  1. Write the formulae of the reactants and the products.
  2. Balance the number of atoms.
  3. Add the charges present.
  4. Add electrons (e⁻) so that the charges on each side balance.

Chloride ions to chlorine gas:
1. $Cl^- \rightarrow Cl_2$
2. $2Cl^- \rightarrow Cl_2$
3. 2^- 0
4. $2Cl^- \rightarrow Cl_2 + 2e^-$

HT Balanced Ionic Equations

* When writing a balanced ionic equation, only the species that actually change form, i.e. gain or lose electrons, are written.
* The species that stay the same, the spectator ions, are ignored.
  1. Write the full balanced equation with state symbols.
  2. Write out all the soluble ionic compounds as separate ions.
  3. Delete everything that appears on both sides of the equation (the spectator ions) to leave the net ionic equation.

lead nitrate + potassium chloride ⟶
                    lead chloride + potassium nitrate

1. $Pb(NO_3)_2(aq) + 2KCl(aq) \longrightarrow PbCl_2(s) + 2KNO_3(aq)$
2. $Pb^{2+}(aq) + 2NO_3^-(aq) + 2K^+(aq) + 2Cl^-(aq) \longrightarrow$
                    $PbCl_2(s) + 2K^+(aq) + 2NO_3^-(aq)$
3. $Pb^{2+}(aq) + 2Cl^-(aq) \longrightarrow PbCl_2(s)$

> **Key Point**
>
> It is convention to show added electrons only; the electrons being taken away are not shown.

> The spectator ions, $NO_3^-(aq)$ and $K^+(aq)$, are removed.

> This is the net ionic equation.

> **Key Words**
>
> cations
> anions
> charge
> limiting reactant
> HT stoichiometry
> HT half equation
> HT species
> HT spectator ions
> HT net ionic equation

Quick Test

1. What are the formulae of barium oxide, copper fluoride and aluminium chloride?
2. Aluminium ions have a charge of 3⁺ and oxide ions have a charge of 2⁻. What is the formula of aluminium oxide?
3. HT What is the net ionic equation for the reaction of $Na_2CO_3(aq) + BaCl_2(aq)$?

Moles and Mass

You must be able to:

- HT Explain what a mole is
- HT Calculate the relative molecular mass, mass and number of moles of substances from equations and experimental results.

Moles

- In chemistry it is important to accurately measure how much of a chemical is present.
- Atoms are very small and there would be too many to count in even 1g of substance.
- Instead a measurement is used that represents a known, precise number of atoms – a mole.
- A mole represents a set amount of substance – the amount of substance that contains the same number of atoms as 12g of the element carbon-12.
- The number of atoms in 1 mole of carbon-12 is a very large number: 6.022×10^{23} atoms.
- This number is known as Avogadro's constant.

HT Key Point

Carbon-12 is the pure isotope of carbon, which has the atomic mass of precisely 12.

Calculations Using Moles

- Every element in the periodic table has an atomic mass.
- This means that the mass of one mole of an element will be equivalent to that element's relative atomic mass in grams (g).
- The mass of one mole of any compound is its relative formula mass (M_r) in g.
- The relative molecular mass of a compound is numerically the same as the relative formula mass. Its units are g/mol.
- You can use the following formulae to calculate the number of moles of an element or compound:

HT Key Point

6.022×10^{23} is written in standard form notation because writing 602 200 000 000 000 000 000 000 is extremely awkward.

$$\text{number of moles} = \frac{\text{mass}}{\text{relative molecular mass}}$$

$$\text{relative molecular mass} = \frac{\text{mass}}{\text{number of moles}}$$

What is the relative molecular mass of magnesium hydroxide, $Mg(OH)_2$?

Mg:	1×24	=	24
O:	2×16	=	32
H:	2×1	=	2
M_r:	$24 + 32 + 2$	=	58

The formula has been given: $Mg(OH)_2$

The relative formula mass of $Mg(OH)_2$ is 58, so the relative molecular mass of $Mg(OH)_2$ is 58g/mol.

How many moles of ethanol are there in 230g of ethanol? (The relative formula mass of ethanol is 46.)

$$\text{number of moles} = \frac{\text{mass}}{\text{relative molecular mass}}$$

$$= \frac{230g}{46g/mol} = 5mol$$

- If the mass of one mole of a chemical is known, then the mass of one atom or molecule can be worked out.

One mole of sulfur has a mass of 32g.
What is the mass of one sulfur atom?

$$\frac{\text{atomic mass of element}}{\text{Avogadro's constant}} = \frac{32g}{6.022 \times 10^{23}} = 5.3 \times 10^{-23}g$$

> **HT** **Key Point**
>
> Showing the units in an equation helps because they cancel out. If the final unit matches what you are trying to find out, you have done the calculation correctly.

Calculating Masses of Reactants or Products

- The ratio of the experimental mass to the atomic mass of the constituent atoms can be used to predict the amount of product in a reaction or vice versa.

How much water will be produced when 2 moles of hydrogen is completely combusted in air?

$$2H_2(g) + O_2(g) \rightarrow 2H_2O(l)$$

relative molar mass of water = $(2 \times 1) + 16 = 18g/mol$
mass of water produced = $2 \times 18 = 36g$

2 moles of hydrogen produce 2 moles of water.

72g of water is produced in the same reaction, how much oxygen was reacted?

$$2H_2(g) + O_2(g) \rightarrow 2H_2O(l)$$

relative molecular mass of water = $(2 \times 1) + 16 = 18g/mol$
relative molecular mass of oxygen = $2 \times 16 = 32g/mol$

moles of water produced = $\frac{72}{18} = 4mol$

moles of oxygen used = 2mol
mass of oxygen used = $2 \times 32 = 64g$

Since 2 moles of water are formed from 1 mole of oxygen, divide by 2.

> **HT** **Key Words**
>
> mole
> carbon-12
> Avogadro's constant
> relative atomic mass
> relative molecular mass

Energetics

You must be able to:

- Explain the difference between endothermic and exothermic reactions
- Draw and label reaction profiles for an endothermic and an exothermic reaction
- Calculate energy changes in a chemical reaction considering bond energies.

Reactions and Temperature

- In a chemical reaction, energy is taken in or given out to the surroundings.
- **Exothermic** reactions release energy to the surroundings causing a temperature rise, e.g. when wood burns through combustion.
- The energy given out by exothermic chemical reactions can be used for heating or to produce electricity, sound or light.
- **Endothermic** reactions absorb energy from the surroundings and cause a temperature drop.
- For example, when ethanoic acid (vinegar) and calcium carbonate react, the temperature of the surroundings decreases.
- Endothermic reactions can be used to make cold packs, which are used for sports injuries.

Key Point

Energy is never lost or used up, it is just transferred.

Activation Energy

- Most of the time chemicals do not spontaneously react.
- A minimum amount of energy is needed to start the reaction. This is called the **activation energy**.
- For example, paper does not normally burn at room temperature.
- To start the combustion reaction, energy has to be added in the form of heat from a match. This provides enough energy to start the reaction.
- As the reaction is exothermic, it will produce enough energy to continue the reaction until all the paper has reacted (burned).

Reaction Profiles

- A graph called a **reaction profile** can be drawn to show the energy changes that take place in exothermic and endothermic reactions.

Energy Change Calculations

- In a chemical reaction:
  - making bonds is an exothermic process (releases energy)
  - breaking bonds is an endothermic process (requires energy).
- Chemical reactions that release more energy by making bonds than breaking them are exothermic reactions.

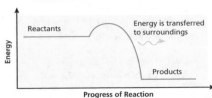

Reaction Profile for an Exothermic Reaction

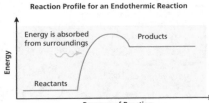

Reaction Profile for an Endothermic Reaction

- That energy was originally stored in the bonds between atoms in the reactants.
- Chemical reactions that need more energy to break bonds than is released when new bonds are made are endothermic reactions.
- The energy taken in from the environment is converted to bond energy between the atoms in the products.
- To work out whether a reaction is exothermic or endothermic, calculations can be carried out using information about how much energy is released when a bond forms and how much energy is needed to break a bond.
- The steps to follow are:
  1. Write out the balanced equation and look at the bonds.
  2. Add up the energies associated with breaking bonds in the reactant(s).
  3. Add up the energies associated with making bonds in the product(s).
  4. Calculate the energy change using the equation below:

 energy change = energy used to break bonds – energy released when new bonds are made

- If the energy change is negative, the reaction is exothermic (more energy is released making bonds than is used breaking them).
- If the energy change is positive, the reaction is endothermic (less energy is released making bonds than is used breaking them).

Hydrogen reacts with iodine to form hydrogen iodide. Calculate the energy change for this reaction.

Bond	Bond Energy (kJ/mol)
H–H	436
I–I	151
H–I	297

$H_2(g) + I_2(g) \rightarrow 2HI(g)$

The reactants contain one H–H bond and one I–I bond. The products contain two H–I bonds.

Total energy needed to break the bonds in
the reactants   = 436 + 151
      = 587kJ/mol

Total energy released making the bonds in
the product   = 2 × 297
      = 594kJ/mol

Energy change   = 587 – 594
      = –7kJ/mol

Energy change is negative, so the reaction is exothermic.

Quick Test

1. What is 'activation energy'?
2. Draw a reaction profile for an endothermic reaction.
3. **HT** The bond making and bond breaking energies in a chemical reaction add up to –15kJ/mol. Is the reaction exothermic or endothermic?

 Key Words

exothermic
endothermic
activation energy
reaction profile
HT environment
HT bond energy

Review Questions

Purity and Separating Mixtures

1 Sanjit is testing a mystery pure substance. He heats the substance until it boils.

    a) How could he confirm the identity of the substance? [2]

    b) Sanjit now takes a sample of water and boils it.
        He finds that the water boils at 101°C.

        Assuming that the thermometer is working correctly, why does the water boil at
        this temperature? [2]

2 What is the empirical formula of each of the following substances?

    a) $C_6H_{12}O_6$ [1]   **b)** CH_3COOH [1]

    c) $CH_3CH_2CH_2COOH$ [1]

3 Calculate the relative formula masses of the following compounds:

    a) $C_6H_{12}O_6$ [1]   **b)** CH_3COOH [1]

    c) CO_2 [1]   **d)** H_2SO_4 [1]

> **Total Marks** _____ / 8

Bonding

1 Which of the following scientists first devised the structure of the modern periodic table?
Circle the correct answer.

    Bohr   Mendel   Mendeleev   Marsden   Rutherford   Thomson [1]

2 Here are the electronic structures of five elements:

Element	Electronic Structure
A	2.1
B	2.8.1
C	2.8.3
D	2.8.8
E	2.2

    a) Which elements are in Period 2 of the periodic table? [2]

    b) Which elements are in the same group? [2]

    c) Which is the most reactive metal? [1]

    d) What is the atomic number of each element? [5]

> **Total Marks** _____ / 11

Models of Bonding

1 Draw a dot and cross diagram to show the covalent bonds in **methane** (CH_4). [2]

2 What advantage do ball and stick models have over dot and cross diagrams? [2]

3 Show, using dot and cross diagrams, how magnesium becomes a magnesium ion. [2]

Total Marks _____ / 6

Properties of Materials

1 Carbon has a number of different **allotropes**.

a) What is meant by the term **allotrope**? [1]

b) Graphite is used as a dry lubricant in air compressors.

Referring to the structure of graphite, explain why it is a good dry lubricant. [4]

c) Diamonds are often used in drill bits.

Referring to the structure of diamond, explain why diamonds are used in drill bits. [3]

d) Give **one** use of graphene. [1]

2 Silver nanoparticles are often impregnated into items such as plastic chopping boards and sticking plasters.

a) Suggest why silver nanoparticles are impregnated into these items. [1]

b) Why are **nanoparticles** so named? [1]

c) Explain why some people are concerned about the risks of using nanoparticles. [2]

3 Which property of nanoparticles makes them suitable for use as a catalyst?
Circle the correct answer: [1]

sized between 1 and 100mm   **small surface area**   **large surface area**   **unreactive**

Total Marks _____ / 14

Practice Questions

Introducing Chemical Reactions

1 What is the **law of conservation of mass**? [1]

2 a) What do the **subscript** numbers that appear after an element symbol mean, e.g. Cl_2? [1]

b) Write the number of atoms of each element shown in each formula below:

i) $C_6H_{12}O_6$ [1]

ii) CH_3CH_2COOH [1]

iii) H_2O_2 [1]

iv) $Ca(NO_3)_2$ [1]

3 Write down the four state symbols. [1]

4 Write the **balanced symbol equations** for the following reactions, including state symbols:

a) magnesium + oxygen → magnesium oxide [2]

b) lithium + oxygen → lithium oxide [2]

c) calcium carbonate + hydrochloric acid → calcium chloride + carbon dioxide + water [2]

d) aluminium + oxygen → aluminium oxide [2]

Total Marks _____ / 15

Chemical Equations

1 What are the charges on these common ions?

a) copper(II) [1]

b) oxide [1]

c) iron(III) [1]

d) sulfide [1]

2. HT Write the half equation for each of the following reactions:

a) Hydrogen ions to hydrogen gas [1]

b) Iron(II) ions to iron solid [1]

c) Copper(II) ions to copper solid [1]

d) Zinc to zinc ions [1]

3. HT Write the ionic equation for the following reaction.
All the compounds involved are soluble, except for silver chloride. [2]

silver nitrate + lithium chloride → lithium nitrate + silver chloride

Total Marks _____ / 10

Moles and Mass

1. HT What does a **mole** represent in chemistry? [1]

2. HT Which of the following is Avogadro's constant?

A 6.022×10^{32} C 3.142×10^{32}

B 6.022×10^{23} D 3.142×10^{23} [1]

3. HT What unit is **molecular mass** measured in? [1]

4. HT Cyanobacteria are organisms that can convert atmospheric nitrogen into nitrates.
Abigail is preparing stock solutions containing different metals to investigate how they affect the growth of cyanobacteria.

42	23
Mo	**V**
molybdenum	vanadium
95.9	50.9

She weighs out 287.7g of the element molybdenum.

a) How many moles of molybdenum does she have?
Show your working. [2]

b) Abigail needs to weigh out 5 moles of vanadium.

What mass of vanadium should she use?
Show your working. [2]

Practice Questions

5 HT What is the relative molecular mass of glucose, $C_6H_{12}O_6$?
(Relative atomic mass of C = 12, H = 1 and O = 16.) [1]

6 HT Calculate the mass of one atom of each of the following elements.
Show your working. Give your answer to one decimal place.

a) Vanadium [2]

b) Molybdenum [2]

c) Caesium [2]

d) Bismuth [2]

7 HT Five moles of hydrogen are completely combusted in air.

How much water is produced in the reaction? [2]

Total Marks _____ / 18

Energetics

1 a) A reaction gives out energy to the environment.

What type of reaction is it? [1]

b) A reaction takes in energy from the environment.

What type of reaction is it? [1]

2 Give **two** ways in which the energy released from a reaction can be used. [2]

3 Explain what is meant by the term **activation energy**. [1]

4 Draw a reaction profile for an exothermic reaction. [1]

5 Draw a reaction profile for an endothermic reaction. [1]

6 HT Which of the following is an **exothermic** process?

making chemical bonds   breaking chemical bonds [1]

7 HT Peter reacted hydrogen gas with fluorine gas to form hydrogen fluoride gas.

The equation for the reaction is: $H_2(g) + F_2(g) \rightarrow 2HF(g)$

Bond	Bond Energy (kJ/mol)
H–F	565
H–H	432
F–F	155

Calculate the energy change for this reaction and state whether the reaction is **exothermic** or **endothermic**. [4]

8 HT A series of reactions was carried out and the energy changes were recorded.

For each energy change, state whether it was **exothermic** or **endothermic**.

a) +90kJ/mol [1]

b) –181kJ/mol [1]

c) +20kJ/mol [1]

d) +8kJ/mol [1]

9 HT Look at the reaction profile for $H_2(g) + F_2(g) \rightarrow 2HF(g)$

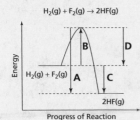

Which letter on the diagram shows the energy change for the reaction? [1]

Total Marks _____ / 17

Types of Chemical Reactions

You must be able to:

- Explain whether a substance is oxidised or reduced in a reaction
- **HT** Explain oxidation and reduction in terms of loss and gain of electrons
- Predict the products of reactions between metals or metal compounds and acids.

Oxidation and Reduction

- When oxygen is added to a substance, it is oxidised.
- When oxygen is removed from a substance, it is reduced.
- The substance that gives away the oxygen is called the oxidising agent.
- The substance that receives the oxygen is the reducing agent.

> **copper oxide + hydrogen ⟶ copper + water**

Copper oxide is the oxidising agent (it loses the oxygen). Hydrogen is the reducing agent (it gains the oxygen to form water).

HT Loss and Gain of Electrons

- Chemists modified the definition of oxidation and reduction when they realised that substances could be oxidised and reduced without oxygen being present.
- The definition now focuses on the loss or gain of electrons in a reaction:
  - If a substance gains electrons, it is reduced.
  - If a substance loses electrons, it is oxidised.

> $$2Na(s) + Cl_2(g) \longrightarrow 2NaCl(s)$$

HT ▶ Key Point

OILRIG: Oxidation Is Loss (of electrons), Reduction Is Gain (of electrons).

Sodium gives away the single electron in its outermost shell, so it has been oxidised. Chlorine receives the electrons from the two sodium atoms, so it has been reduced.

Acids and Alkalis

- When an acid or alkali is dissolved in water, the ions that make up the substance move freely.
  - An acid produces hydrogen ions, $H^+(aq)$.
  - An alkali produces hydroxide / hydroxyl ions, $OH^-(aq)$.
- For example, a solution of hydrochloric acid, HCl, will dissociate into $H^+(aq)$ and $Cl^-(aq)$ ions.
- A solution of sodium hydroxide, NaOH, will dissociate into $Na^+(aq)$ and $OH^-(aq)$ ions.

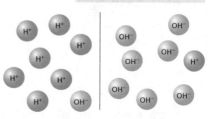

low pH = lots of H^+ lots of OH^- = high pH

Neutralisation

- Neutralisation occurs when an acid reacts with an alkali or a base, to form a salt and water.

> **acid + base ⟶ salt + water**

- For example, hydrochloric acid reacts with sodium hydroxide to produce sodium chloride and water:

$$HCl(aq) + NaOH(aq) \longrightarrow NaCl(aq) + H_2O(l)$$

- The reaction can be rewritten to only show the species that change:

$$H^+(aq) + OH^-(aq) \longrightarrow H_2O(l)$$

Reacting Metals with Acid

- Many metals will react in the presence of an acid to form a salt and hydrogen gas.

> **metal + acid $\longrightarrow$ salt + hydrogen**

- The reactivity of a metal determines whether it will react with an acid and how vigorously it reacts.
- Metals can be arranged in order of reactivity in a reactivity series.
- If there is a reaction, then the name of the salt produced is based on the acid used:
  - Hydrochloric acid forms chlorides.
  - Nitric acid forms nitrates.
  - Sulfuric acid forms sulfates.

magnesium + hydrochloric acid $\longrightarrow$
      magnesium chloride + hydrogen
$$Mg(s) + 2HCl(aq) \longrightarrow MgCl_2(aq) + H_2(g)$$

Reacting Metal Carbonates with Acid

- Metal carbonates also react with acids to form a metal salt, plus water and carbon dioxide gas.

> **metal carbonate + acid $\longrightarrow$**
>   **salt + water + carbon dioxide**

- The salts produced are named in the same way as for metals reacting with acids.

magnesium carbonate + sulfuric acid $\longrightarrow$
      magnesium sulfate + water + carbon dioxide
$$MgCO_3(s) + H_2SO_4(aq) \longrightarrow MgSO_4(aq) + H_2O(l) + CO_2(aq)$$

> ## Key Point
>
> Remember, ionic substances separate from each other when dissolved or molten. The ions move freely and are not joined together.

> ## Key Point
>
> Water is not an ionic compound. It is a polar molecule (it has positively charged hydrogen and negatively charged oxygen), which means that ionic substances can dissolve easily into it.

Reactivity Series

Most Reactive

The higher the metal is positioned the more readily it reacts with oxygen. This is useful for protecting metals lower down against corrosion. $\rightarrow$

Sodium
Calcium
Magnesium
Aluminium

These metals slowly react with oxygen and corrode away.

Zinc
Iron

This metal will very slightly discolour to show oxygen has had very little effect. It very rarely corrodes. $\rightarrow$

Lead
Copper

These metals remain unaffected by oxygen. $\rightarrow$

Gold
Platinum

Least Reactive

> ## Key Words
>
> oxidised
> reduced
> oxidising agent
> reducing agent
> acid
> alkali
> neutralisation
> base
> salt

Quick Test

1. What gas is made when metal carbonates react with acid?
2. What salt is made when zinc oxide is reacted with nitric acid?
3. Write the word equation for the reaction between copper oxide and sulfuric acid.

pH, Acids and Neutralisation

You must be able to:

- Describe techniques to measure pH
- **HT** Explain the terms dilute, concentrated, weak and strong in relation to acids
- **HT** Explain pH in terms of dissociation of ions.

Measuring pH

- Indicators change colour depending on whether they are in acidic or alkaline solutions.
- Single indicators, such as litmus, produce a sudden colour change when there is a change from acid to alkali or vice versa.
- pH is a scale from 0 to 14 that provides a measure of how acidic or alkaline a solution is.
- Universal indicator is a mixture of different indicators, which gives a continuous range of colours.
- The pH of a solution can be estimated by comparing the colour of the indicator in solution to a pH colour chart.

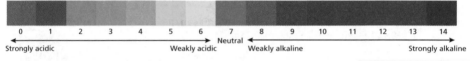

| 0 | 1 | 2 | 3 | 4 | 5 | 6 | 7 | 8 | 9 | 10 | 11 | 12 | 13 | 14 |

Neutral

Strongly acidic　　　　　　　Weakly acidic　　Weakly alkaline　　　　　　Strongly alkaline

- pH can also be measured electronically using an electronic data logger with a pH probe, which gives the numerical value of the pH.

Key Point

Judging something using the eye is a qualitative measurement and has more variation than a quantitative measurement, such as a pH reading from a pH probe.

HT Dilute and Concentrated Acids

- Acids can be dilute or concentrated.
- The degree of dilution depends upon the amount of acid dissolved in a volume of water.
- The higher the ratio of acid to water in a solution, the higher the concentration.
- Acids dissociate (split apart) into their component ions when dissolved in solution.
- The concentration is measured as the number of moles of acid per cubic decimetre of water (mol/dm³).
- For example, 1mol/dm³ is less concentrated than 2mol/dm³ of the same acid.

Key Point

Don't confuse the term 'concentrated' with how 'strong' an acid or alkali is.

HT Strong and Weak Acids

- The terms weak acid and strong acid refer to how well an acid dissociates into ions in solution.
- Strong acids easily form H⁺ ions.

$$HCl(aq) \longrightarrow H^+(aq) + Cl^-(aq)$$
$$HNO_3(aq) \longrightarrow H^+(aq) + NO_3^-(aq)$$
$$H_2SO_4(aq) \longrightarrow 2H^+(aq) + SO_4^{2-}(aq)$$

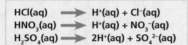

- These strong acids fully ionise.
- Acids that do not fully ionise form an *equilibrium mixture*.
- This means that the ions that are formed can recombine into the original acid. For example:

| ethanoic acid $\rightleftharpoons$ ethanoate ions + hydrogen ions |
| $CH_3COOH(aq) \rightleftharpoons CH_3COO^-(aq)$ + $H^+(aq)$ |

Concentrated weak acid – a lot of acid present, but little dissociation of acid

Concentrated strong acid – a lot of acid present with a lot of dissociation to form many hydrogen ions

acid (HA) $\rightleftharpoons$ hydrogen ion (H^+) + anion (A^-)

HT Changing pH

- pH is a measure of how many hydrogen ions are in solution.
- Changing the concentration of an acid leads to a change in pH.
- The more concentrated the acid, the lower the pH and vice versa.
- The concentration of hydrogen ions will be greater in a strong acid compared to a weak acid.
- The pH of a strong acid will therefore be lower than the equivalent concentration of weak acid.
- As the concentration of H^+ ions increases by a factor of 10, the pH decreases by one unit.
- A solution of an acid with a pH of 4 has 10 times more H^+ ions than a solution with a pH of 5.
- A solution of an acid with a pH of 3 has 100 times more H^+ ions than a solution with a pH of 5.

Dilute weak acid – little acid present with little dissociation of acid

Dilute strong acid – little acid present but with a high degree of dissociation

HT Neutralisation and pH

- For neutralisation to occur, the number of H^+ ions must exactly cancel the number of OH^- ions.
- pH curves can be drawn to show what happens to the pH in a neutralisation reaction:
  - An acid has a low pH – when an alkali is added to it, the pH increases.
  - An alkali has a high pH – when an acid is added to it, the pH decreases.
- You should be able to read and interpret pH curves (like the one opposite) to work out:
  - the volume of acid needed to neutralise the alkali
  - the pH after a certain amount of acid has been added.

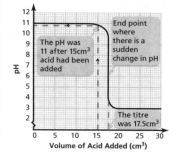

Quick Test

1. Why can universal indicator be more useful than litmus indicator?
2. HT What two pieces of information can a pH curve tell you about an acid or alkali?
3. HT What is pH a measure of?

Key Words

pH
HT dilute
HT concentrated
HT dissociate
HT weak acid
HT strong acid
HT equilibrium mixture

Electrolysis

You must be able to:

- Predict the products of electrolysis of simple ionic compounds in the molten state
- Describe the competing reactions in the electrolysis of aqueous compounds
- Describe electrolysis in terms of the ions present and the reactions at the electrodes
- Describe the technique of electrolysis using inert and non-inert electrodes

Electrolysis

- Ionic compounds can be broken down into their constituent elements using electricity. The substance being broken down is known as the electrolyte. The electrolyte must be molten or dissolved in water so that the ions can move and conduct electricity.
- Electrodes are made of solid materials that conduct electricity.
- The positively charged electrode is called the anode.
- The negatively charged electrode is called the cathode.
- During electrolysis, cations (positively charged ions) are attracted to the cathode and anions (negatively charged ions) to the anode.

Electrolysis of Molten Compounds, e.g. NaCl

- During the electrolysis of molten sodium chloride, the cations (sodium ions) are attracted to the cathode. Here they gain electrons and turn into sodium atoms.
- Metallic sodium can be seen to form at the cathode.

HT This is a reduction reaction. A reduction reaction occurs when a species gains electrons.

HT This process can be shown by writing a half-equation.

HT **At the cathode:**
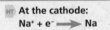
$$Na^+ + e^- \longrightarrow Na$$

- The anions (chloride ions) are attracted to the anode. Here each chloride ion loses an electron, to form a chlorine atom. Two chlorine atoms pair up to form a chlorine molecule.

HT This is an oxidation reaction. An oxidation reaction occurs when a species loses electrons.

HT The half-equation for this reaction is

HT **At the anode:**
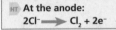
$$2Cl^- \longrightarrow Cl_2 + 2e^-$$

- Chlorine gas can be seen to form at the anode.
- The electrons produced at the anode are pumped by the battery through the wires in the circuit to the cathode, where they are given to the sodium ions.

> **Key Point**
>
> Unless the ions can move (i.e. the substance is in solution or molten) electrolysis will not occur.

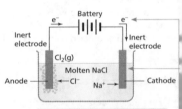

Electrolysis of molten sodium chloride takes place when the compound is heated beyond its melting point (801°C).

Na(s) forming on surface of cathode.

This is a reduction process as electrons are gained.

This is an oxidation process as electrons are lost.

- The products of molten binary ionic compounds (i.e. ionic compounds made up of two elements) will always be the two elements present in the compound. The metal will always be formed at the cathode and the non-metal at the anode.

Electrolysis of Aqueous Solutions, e.g. $CuSO_4$ (aq)

- Aqueous solutions contain cations and anions from the ionic compound dissolved in the water.
- They also contain H^+ ions and OH^- ions from the water.
- This means the ions shown in the table alongside are present in copper sulfate solution.
- Only one ion is attracted to each electrode.
- At the cathode 'the least reactive element is formed'.
- Copper is below hydrogen in the reactivity series and so will be formed at the cathode.

HT The half-equation for this reaction is $Cu^{2+} + 2e^- \longrightarrow Cu$

- When inert (non-reactive) electrodes are used, the product at the cathode is always a metal or hydrogen (if hydrogen is less reactive than the metal that is also present).
- At the anode 'oxygen is formed unless a halogen (group 7) ion is present'.
- In the electrolysis of copper sulfate solution, there are no halogen ions present so oxygen is formed at the anode.

HT The half-equation for this reaction is $4OH^- \longrightarrow O_2 + 2H_2O + 4e^-$

- The H^+ ions and SO_4^{2-} ions are unaffected and remain in solution.
- Non-metals are always formed at the anode when inert electrodes are used.

Use of Inert and Non-Inert Electrodes

- Inert electrodes do not react during electrolysis.
- Typically they are made from carbon.
- Electrodes can be made out of inert metals instead, such as platinum, which will not react with the products of electrolysis. But, platinum electrodes are very expensive.
- Non-inert or active electrodes can be used for processes such as electroplating, e.g. using copper electrodes with copper sulfate solution.
- In the electrolysis here, if the cathode were replaced with a metal object it would become covered in copper metal, i.e. it will be copper-plated.

Electrolysis of Copper Sulfate Solution

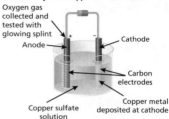

Oxygen gas collected and tested with glowing splint

Anode

Cathode

Carbon electrodes

Copper metal deposited at cathode

Copper sulfate solution

Cations Present	Anions Present
Cu^{2+}	SO_4^{2-}
H^+	OH^-

Key Point

Ionic solutions conduct electricity because the ions that make up the solution move to the electrodes, *not* because electrons move through the solution.

Active Electrodes

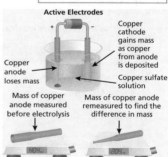

Copper cathode gains mass as copper from anode is deposited

Copper anode loses mass

Copper sulfate solution

Mass of copper anode measured before electrolysis

Mass of copper anode remeasured to find the difference in mass

Key Words

electrolyte
anode
cathode
electrolysis
cations
anions
inert electrode
active electrode

Quick Test

1. Name the products of electrolysis of **molten** magnesium bromide.
2. Name the products of electrolysis of **aqueous** magnesium bromide.
3. HT During the electrolysis of molten aluminium oxide, aluminium is formed from aluminium ions. Write a half-equation to show this reaction.

Review Questions

Introducing Chemical Reactions

1 Write down the number of atoms of each element in each of the following compounds.

   a) H_2SO_4 [1]

   b) $Cu(NO_3)_2$ [1]

   c) CH_3CH_2COOH [1]

   d) C_2H_6 [1]

2 Balance the following equations:

   a) $CuO(s) + H_2SO_4(aq) \rightarrow CuSO_4(aq) + H_2O(l)$ [2]

   b) $Mg(s) + O_2(g) \rightarrow MgO(s)$ [2]

   c) $Mg(OH)_2(aq) + HCl(aq) \rightarrow MgCl_2(aq) + H_2O(l)$ [2]

   d) $CH_4(g) + O_2(g) \rightarrow CO_2(g) + H_2O(l)$ [2]

3 The table below shows the names and formulae of some common ions.

Fill in the missing information to complete the table.

Name of Ion	Formula
Carbonate	
Lithium	
	Fe^{3+}
	O^{2-}
Sulfate	

[5]

4 HT Write the half equation for each of the following reactions:

   a) Solid lead to lead ions [1]

   b) Aluminium ions to aluminium [1]

   c) Bromine to bromide ions [1]

   d) Silver ions to solid silver [1]

Total Marks _____ / 21

Chemical Equations

1 HT When writing a balanced ionic equation, which species appear in the equation? [1]

2 HT Write the net ionic equation for:

HT **a)** $AgNO_3(aq) + KCl(aq) \rightarrow AgCl(s) + KNO_3(aq)$ [1]

b) magnesium nitrate (aq) + sodium carbonate (aq) →
magnesium carbonate (s) + sodium nitrate (aq) [1]

Total Marks _____ / 3

Moles and Mass

1 HT Calculate the **number of moles** of each of the following elements:

a) 6.9g of Li [1]

b) 62g of P [1]

2 HT Calculate the molar mass of ammonium chloride, NH_4Cl.
(The relative atomic mass of H = 1, Cl = 35.5 and N = 14.) [1]

3 HT Calculate the mass of one atom of each of the following elements.
Use the periodic table on page 48 to help you.

a) Tungsten [1]

b) Tin [1]

4 HT Barium chloride reacts with magnesium sulfate to produce barium sulfate and magnesium chloride.

What mass of barium sulfate will be produced if 5mol of barium chloride completely reacts?
Show your working. [2]

Review Questions

5 HT How many moles are there in 22g of butanoic acid, $C_4H_8O_2$?

A 0.1   C 0.5

B 0.25   D 1   [1]

Total Marks _____ / 8

Energetics

1 Atu pulls a muscle whilst playing rugby.
A cold pack is applied to his leg to help cool the muscle and prevent further injury.
The pack contains ammonium nitrate and water.
When the pack is crushed, the two chemicals mix and ammonium nitrate
dissolves endothermically.

a) What is meant by the term **endothermic**?   [1]

b) Where does the energy come from that enables the pack to work?   [1]

2 HT Mark reacts hydrogen gas with chlorine gas:

$H_2(g) + Cl_2(g) \rightarrow 2HCl(g)$

Bond	Bond Energies (kJ/mol)
H–Cl	431
H–H	436
Cl–Cl	243

a) Calculate the energy change for the reaction and state whether the reaction is
   endothermic or **exothermic**.   [3]

b) Draw the expected reaction profile for the reaction.   [1]

Total Marks _____ / 6

Types of Chemical Reactions

1 Which reactions involve a reactant being oxidised? [2]

A magnesium + oxygen → magnesium oxide

B water (solid) → water (liquid)

C copper + oxygen → copper oxide

D barium carbonate + sodium sulfate → barium sulfate + sodium carbonate

2 HT Explain what oxidation and reduction mean in terms of electrons. [2]

3 For each of the following reactions, write a balanced equation, including state symbols. Then state which species has been oxidised and which has been reduced.

a) sodium + chlorine → sodium chloride [3]

b) magnesium + oxygen → magnesium oxide [3]

c) lithium + bromine → lithium bromide [3]

d) copper(II) oxide + hydrogen → copper + water [3]

4 What ions are produced by:

a) An acid? [1]

b) An alkali? [1]

5 What is the general equation for the neutralisation of a base by an acid? [1]

6 Dilute sulfuric acid and sodium hydroxide solution are reacted together.

a) Write the balanced symbol equation for the reaction. [2]

b) Which ions are not involved in the reaction? [2]

c) HT Write the ionic equation for the reaction between dilute sulfuric acid and sodium hydroxide solution. [2]

Total Marks _____ / 25

Practice Questions

pH, Acids and Neutralisation

1 HT What is meant by the term **weak acid**? [1]

2 HT Look at the concentrations below. For each pair, which is more concentrated?

a) $1mol/dm^3$ H_2SO_4 OR $2mol/dm^3$ H_2SO_4 [1]

b) $3mol/dm^3$ HNO_3 OR $2mol/dm^3$ HNO_3 [1]

3 HT How many more times concentrated are the H^+ ions in a solution with a pH of 6 compared to a solution with a pH of 3? [1]

Total Marks _____ / 4

Electrolysis

1 What are the ions of **a)** metals and **b)** non-metals called? [2]

2 What is **electrolysis**? [1]

3 Why is it not possible to carry out electrolysis on crystals of table salt (sodium chloride) at room temperature and pressure? [1]

4 Describe how you could copper-plate a nail using copper(II) sulfate solution. [3]

5 a) Why are inert electrodes often used in electrolysis? [1]

b) Platinum can be used as an inert electrode. However, they are rarely used.

Why are platinum electrodes rarely used? [1]

Total Marks _____ / 9

Types of Chemical Reactions

1 Which **two** of the following reactions are oxidation reactions?

    A aluminium + oxygen → aluminium oxide

    B sodium chloride + silver nitrate → silver chloride + sodium nitrate

    C copper sulfate + sodium hydroxide → copper hydroxide + sodium sulfate

    D copper + oxygen → copper oxide   [2]

2 Look at the following reaction:

iron(III) oxide + carbon monoxide → iron + carbon dioxide

    a) Which species is being **reduced**?   [1]

    b) Which species is being **oxidised**?   [1]

    c) Write the balanced symbol equation for the reaction.   [2]

3 HT Claudia places a copper wire into a solution of colourless silver nitrate solution.

Time ⟶

As time passes, Claudia notices that shiny crystals start developing on the surface of the copper wire.
She also notices that the solution becomes a light blue colour.

    a) Write the balanced symbol equation for the reaction between copper and silver nitrate.   [2]

    b) What are the shiny crystals on the wire?   [1]

Review Questions

c) What causes the blue coloration of the solution? [1]

d) Which chemical species are being oxidised and which are being reduced?
You must explain your answer. [2]

Total Marks _____ / 12

pH, Acids and Neutralisation

1 Underline the **acid** in each reaction.

a) $Mg(OH)_2(aq) + 2HCl(aq) \rightarrow MgCl_2(aq) + 2H_2O(l)$ [1]

b) $H_2SO_4(aq) + 2NaOH(aq) \rightarrow Na_2SO_4(aq) + 2H_2O(l)$ [1]

c) $2CH_3COOH(aq) + 2Na(s) \rightarrow H_2(g) + 2CH_3COONa(aq)$ [1]

d) $2HF(aq) + Mg(s) \rightarrow MgF_2(aq) + H_2(g)$ [1]

2 Part of the reactivity series is shown in the diagram on the right.
When a metal is reacted with an acid it forms a metal salt, plus hydrogen
gas. For example:

lead + sulfuric acid → lead sulfate + hydrogen

calcium + sulfuric acid → calcium sulfate + hydrogen

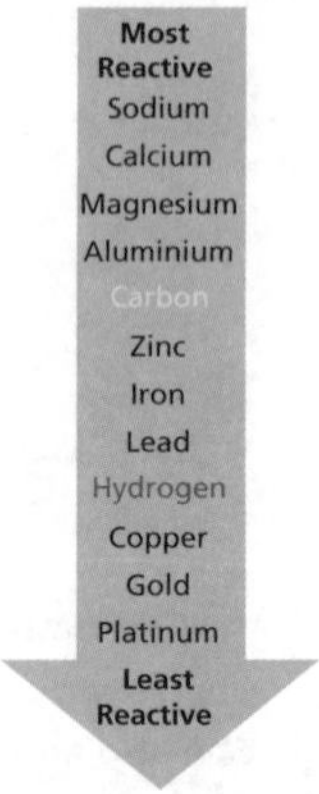

a) Which of the two reactions has the fastest initial reaction? [1]

b) A metal **X** is reacted with sulfuric acid.
It reacts violently compared with the other two reactions.

Where would **X** be placed on the reactivity series? [1]

Reactivity Series

Most Reactive
Sodium
Calcium
Magnesium
Aluminium
Carbon
Zinc
Iron
Lead
Hydrogen
Copper
Gold
Platinum
Least Reactive

3 Nitric acid and sodium hydroxide are reacted together.

a) Write the balanced symbol equation for the reaction. [2]

b) Which ions are spectator ions? [2]

c) Rewrite the equation you wrote for part a) showing only the reacting species. [2]

4 HT What is meant by the term **strong acid**? [1]

5 How many more times concentrated are the H^+ ions in a solution with a pH of 6 compared to a solution with a pH of 2? [1]

> **Total Marks** _____ / 14

Electrolysis

1 In what state(s) will ionic compounds conduct electricity? [1]

2 Masum is carrying out the electrolysis of water and sulfuric acid.

a) Which of the following would be the most appropriate material for the electrodes?

   A Wood

   B Copper

   C Carbon

   D Plastic [1]

b) Write the names of the anions and cations involved in this electrolysis. [2]

c) Write the reactions taking place at **i)** the anode and **ii)** the cathode. [2]

3 Electrolysis is used to copper-plate objects.

The diagram below shows the apparatus for electroplating using copper and a metal object in copper(II) sulfate solution.

What are ions **X** and **Y**? [2]

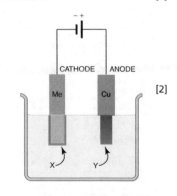

> **Total Marks** _____ / 8

Answers

Page 5 Quick Test
1. 58.3 g
2. Mixtures of substances in solution
3. CH_3

Page 7 Quick Test
1. By atomic number; by number of electrons in the outermost shell
2. Magnesium, 2.8.2

3. 2.8.7

Page 9 Quick Test
1. The electrons in the outermost shells of the metal atoms are free to move, so there are a large number of electrons moving between the metal ions
2. **Any two from:** Distances between electrons and the nucleus are not realistic; bonds appear to be physical structures; bond lengths are not in proportion to the size of the atom; they do not give a good idea of the 3D shape of the atoms
3. A 3D arrangement of a large number of repeating units (molecules / atoms) joined together by covalent bonds

Page 11 Quick Test
1. A compound that contains carbon
2. It is a giant covalent molecule in which every carbon atom forms bonds with four other carbon atoms (the maximum number of bonds possible)
3. 1–100nm

Page 12 Purity and Separating Mixtures
1. a) Containing one type of atom or molecule only **[1]**
   b) Every substance has a specific melting point at room temperature and pressure **[1]**; if the substance melts at a different temperature, it indicates that there are impurities **[1]**
2. a) Distance moved by the solvent = 28 **[1]**; $R_f =$
   $$\frac{\text{distance moved by the compound}}{\text{distance moved by the solvent}},$$
   R_f (pink) $= \frac{7.5}{28} = 0.27$ **[1]**;
   R_f (purple) $= \frac{17.5}{28} = 0.63$ **[1]**
   b) D **[1]**
3. $C = \frac{84}{12} = 7$ **[1]**; $H = \frac{16}{1} = 16$, $O = \frac{64}{16} = 4$ **[1]**;
   $C_7H_{16}O_4$ **[1]**

   Look for common factors to see whether an empirical formula can be simplified further.

Page 12 Bonding
1. a) H = 1, Na = 11, Mg = 12, C = 6, O = 8, K = 19, Ca = 20, Al = 13 **[2]** (1 mark for 6–7 correct; 0 marks for 5 or less correct)
   b) (2 × 39.1) + 16 = 94.1 **[1]** (Accept 94)
   c) 16 × 2 = 32 **[1]**
2. a) C **[1]**
   b) B = 2.8.1 **[1]**; E = 2.8.7 **[1]**
   c) Electrons **[1]**

Page 13 Models of Bonding
1. a) An atom or molecule that has gained or lost electrons **[1]**
   b) A correctly drawn sodium ion (2.8) **[1]**; and chloride ion (2.8.8) **[1]**

Sodium ion, Na^+ Chloride ion, Cl^-

2. a) A bond formed by the sharing **[1]**; of two outer electrons **[1]**
   b) Two correctly drawn chlorine atoms (each with 7 electrons) **[1]**; overlapping and sharing two electrons **[1]**

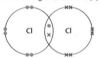

Page 13 Properties of Materials
1. a) **Any three from:** Carbon has four electrons in its outer shell **[1]**; it can form covalent bonds **[1]**; with up to four other atoms **[1]**; and can form chains **[1]**
   b) An allotrope is a different form of an element **[1]**
   c) **Any three from:** graphite **[1]**; diamond **[1]**; fullerene / buckminsterfullerene **[1]**; graphene **[1]**; lonsdaleite **[1]**; amorphous carbon **[1]**
2. a) It conducts electricity because it has free electrons **[1]**; and it is stronger than steel **[1]**
   b) Diamond does not conduct electricity **[1]**
   c) A diagram showing each carbon joined to four other carbon atoms **[1]**; with a minimum of five atoms shown in tetrahedral arrangement **[1]**

Diamond

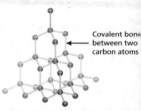

Covalent bond between two carbon atoms

3. a) The ions must be either molten **[1]**; or dissolved in aqueous solution **[1]**
   b) In crystalline form, the distance between the ions is at its smallest / the ions are close together **[1]**; so the electrostatic forces are very high and have to be overcome for the crystal to melt **[1]**

Page 15 Quick Test
1. $Ca(OH)_2$
2. $2Na(s) + Cl_2(g) \rightarrow 2NaCl(s)$
3. $2Mg, 2S, 8O$ ($2 \times O_4$)

Page 17 Quick Test
1. BaO, CuF_2, $AlCl_3$
2. Al_2O_3
3. $Ba^{2+}(aq) + CO_3^{2-}(aq) \rightarrow BaCO_3(s)$

   The $BaCO_3$ formed is insoluble.

Page 19 Quick Test
1. mass = number of moles × relative molecular mass
2. 18g
3. $2.2 \times 10^{-22}g$

Page 21 Quick Test
1. The minimum amount of energy needed to start a reaction
2.

Reaction Profile for an Endothermic Reaction

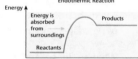

3. Exothermic

Page 22 Purity and Separating Mixtures
1. a) Measure its boiling point **[1]**; compare the boiling point with data from a data book / known values **[1]**
   b) The water is not pure **[1]**; it contains other substances **[1]**
2. a) CH_2O **[1]**

In $C_6H_{12}O_6$ the common factor of all the numbers is 6, so divide by six to simplify the formula.

b) CH_2O **[1]**

Collect all the atoms of the same element together first, and then simplify: $CH_3COOH \rightarrow C_2H_4O_2 \rightarrow CH_2O$

c) C_2H_4O **[1]**
a) $(6 \times 12) + (12 \times 1) + (6 \times 16) = 180$ **[1]**
b) $(2 \times 12) + (4 \times 1) + (2 \times 16) = 60$ **[1]**
c) $(1 \times 12) + (2 \times 16) = 44$ **[1]**
d) $(2 \times 1) + (32.1) + (4 \times 16) = 98.1$ **[1]** (Accept 98)

ge 22 Bonding
Mendeleev **[1]**
a) A **[1]**; E **[1]**
b) A **[1]**; B **[1]**
c) B **[1]**
d) A = 3 **[1]**; B = 11 **[1]**; C = 13 **[1]**; D = 18 **[1]**; E = 4 **[1]**

ge 23 Models of Bonding
One carbon atom drawn **[1]**; with covalent bonds with four hydrogen atoms **[1]**

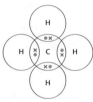

Ball and stick models give a better picture of the 3D shape of the molecule **[1]**; and the bond angles / directions **[1]**
A correctly drawn magnesium atom, 2.8.2 **[1]**; and magnesium ion $(2.8)^{2+}$ **[1]**

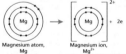

Magnesium atom, Mg   Magnesium ion, Mg^{2+}

ge 23 Properties of Materials
a) A different physical structure to other forms of the element **[1]**
b) Graphite is made of layers of atoms **[1]**; these are held together by weak forces **[1]**; so the layers can separate / slide over each other easily **[1]**; preventing the surfaces from rubbing together **[1]**
c) In diamond all possible covalent bonds have been used / each carbon atom is bonded to four other carbon atoms **[1]**; so it is extremely hard **[1]**; and has a high melting point **[1]**

You need to mention high melting point so the third mark. Drill bits get hot due to frictional forces, so it is an important property.

d) **Any one from:** electrical components **[1]**; solar panels **[1]**
2. a) Silver has antibacterial properties **[1]**
b) They are 1–100nm in size (in the nanometre range) **[1]**
c) **Any two from:** they can easily get into the human body / cells / the environment **[1]**; they can catalyse reactions **[1]**; they can kill good bacteria **[1]**; the effect on the human immune system is not known **[1]**
3. large surface area **[1]**

Page 24 Introducing Chemical Reactions
1. In a chemical reaction, the mass of the reactants will always equal to the mass of the products **[1]** (Accept: No atoms are made or destroyed)
2. a) The number of atoms of that element present (the element before the number) **[1]**
b) i) C = 6, H = 12, O = 6 **[1]**
ii) C = 3, H = 6, O = 2 **[1]**
iii) H = 2, O = 2 **[1]**
iv) Ca = 1, N = 2, O = 6 **[1]**
3. solid = (s), liquid = (l), gas = (g), aqueous = (aq) **[1]**
4. a) $2Mg(s) + O_2(g) \rightarrow 2MgO(s)$ **[2]** (1 mark for correct balancing; 1 mark for correct state symbols)
b) $4Li(s) + O_2(g) \rightarrow 2Li_2O(s)$ **[2]** (1 mark for correct balancing; 1 mark for correct state symbols)
c) $CaCO_3(s) + 2HCl(aq) \rightarrow CaCl_2(aq) + CO_2(g) + H_2O(l)$ **[2]** (1 mark for correct balancing; 1 mark for correct state symbols)
d) $4Al(s) + 3O_2(g) \rightarrow 2Al_2O_3(s)$ **[2]** (1 mark for correct balancing; 1 mark for correct state symbols)

Page 24 Chemical Equations
1. a) 2+ **[1]**
b) 2– **[1]**
c) 3+ **[1]**
d) 2– **[1]**
2. a) $2H^+(aq) + 2e^- \rightarrow H_2(g)$ **[1]**
b) $Fe^{2+}(aq) + 2e^- \rightarrow Fe(s)$ **[1]**
c) $Cu^{2+}(aq) + 2e^- \rightarrow Cu(s)$ **[1]**
d) $Zn(s) \rightarrow Zn^{2+}(aq) + 2e^-$ **[1]**
3. $Ag^+(aq) + Cl^-(aq) \rightarrow AgCl(s)$ **[2]** (1 mark for the correct ions and product; 1 mark for the correct charges)

Page 25 Moles and Mass
1. One mole of a substance contains the same number of particles as the number of atoms in 12g of the element carbon-12 **[1]**
2. B **[1]**

3. g/mol **[1]**
4. a) number of moles of Mo = $\frac{mass}{relative\ molecular\ mass}$ = $\frac{287.7g}{95.9g/mol}$ **[1]**; = 3mol **[1]**
b) mass = relative molecular mass × number of moles = 50.9g/mol × 5 mol **[1]**; = 254.5g **[1]** (Accept 255g)

Rearrange the equation
$moles = \frac{mass}{relative\ molecular\ mass}$
to work out the mass.

5. $(6 \times 12) + (12 \times 1) + (6 \times 16) = 180$ **[1]**
6. a) mass of one atom (V) = $\frac{atomic\ mass}{Avogadro's\ constant} = \frac{50.9g}{6.022 \times 10^{23}}$ **[1]**; = 8.5×10^{-23}g **[1]**
b) mass of one atom (Mo) = $\frac{95.9g}{6.022 \times 10^{23}}$ **[1]**; = 1.6×10^{-22}g **[1]**
c) mass of one atom (Cs) = $\frac{132.9g}{6.022 \times 10^{23}}$ **[1]**; = 2.2×10^{-22}g **[1]**
d) mass of one atom (Bi) = $\frac{209g}{6.022 \times 10^{23}}$ **[1]**; = 3.5×10^{-22}g **[1]**
7. $2H_2(g) + O_2(g) \rightarrow 2H_2O(l)$, 1mol of $H_2 \rightarrow$ 1mol of H_2O, so 5mol of $H_2 \rightarrow$ 5mol of H_2O **[1]**; 1mol of $H_2O = (2 \times 1) + 16 = 18$g, so 5mol of $H_2O = 5 \times 18 = 90$g **[1]**

Page 26 Energetics
1. a) Exothermic **[1]**
b) Endothermic **[1]**
2. **Any two from:** heating (water / central heating) **[1]**; produce electricity **[1]**; make sound **[1]**; make light **[1]**
3. The minimum energy required to start a reaction **[1]**
4. A correctly drawn reaction profile for an exothermic reaction **[1]**

5. A correctly drawn reaction profile for an endothermic reaction **[1]**

6. making chemical bonds **[1]**
7. Bond breaking: 432 + 155 = 587kJ/mol

Answers

[1]; bond making: 2 × 565 = 1130kJ/mol [1]; bond breaking – bond making (ΔH) = 587 – 1130 = –543kJ/mol [1]; the reaction is exothermic [1]

8.
a) Endothermic [1]
b) Exothermic [1]
c) Endothermic [1]
d) Endothermic [1]

9. C [1]

Pages 28–33 Revise Questions

Page 29 Quick Test
1. Carbon dioxide
2. Zinc nitrate
3. copper oxide + sulfuric acid → copper sulfate + water

Page 31 Quick Test
1. Universal indicator can show a range of pHs from 1 to 14. Litmus paper only shows if something is an acid or alkali.
2. The volume of acid needed to neutralise the alkali; the pH when a certain amount of acid has been added.
3. pH is a measure of the number of H^+ ions in solution.

Page 33 Quick Test
1. Magnesium will be formed at the cathode and bromine at the anode.
2. Hydrogen will be formed at the cathode and bromine at the anode.
3. $Al^{3+} + 3e^- \rightarrow Al$

Pages 34–36 Review Questions

Page 34 Introducing Chemical Reactions
1.
a) H = 2, S = 1, O = 4 [1]
b) Cu = 1, N = 2, O = 6 [1]
c) C = 3, H = 6, O = 2 [1]
d) C = 2, H = 6 [1]

2.
a) $CuO(s) + H_2SO_4(aq) \rightarrow CuSO_4(aq) + H_2O(l)$ [2]
(1 mark for correct reactants; 1 mark for correct products)
b) $2Mg(s) + O_2(g) \rightarrow 2MgO(s)$ [2]
(1 mark for correct reactants; 1 mark for correct products)
c) $Mg(OH)_2(aq) + 2HCl(aq) \rightarrow MgCl_2(aq) + 2H_2O(l)$ [2]
(1 mark for correct reactants; 1 mark for correct products)
d) $CH_4(g) + 2O_2(g) \rightarrow CO_2(g) + 2H_2O(l)$ [2]
(1 mark for correct reactants; 1 mark for correct products)

3.

Name of Ion	Formula
Carbonate	CO_3^{2-} [1]
Lithium	Li^+ [1]
Iron(III) [1]	Fe^{3+}
Oxide [1]	O^{2-}
Sulfate	SO_4^{2-} [1]

4.
a) $Pb(s) \rightarrow Pb^{2+}(aq / l) + 2e^-$ [1]
b) $Al^{3+}(aq / l) + 3e^- \rightarrow Al(s)$ [1]
c) $Br_2(l) + 2e^- \rightarrow 2Br^-(aq)$ [1]
d) $Ag^+(aq) + e^- \rightarrow Ag(s)$ [1]

Page 35 Chemical Equations
1. The reacting species [1]

Spectator ions are not included in ionic equations.

2.
a) $Ag^+(aq) + Cl^-(aq) \rightarrow AgCl(s)$ [1]
b) $Mg^{2+}(aq) + CO_3^{2-}(aq) \rightarrow MgCO_3(s)$ [1]

Page 35 Moles and Mass
1.
a) $\frac{6.9g}{6.9g/mol} = 1mol$ [1]
b) $\frac{62g}{31g/mol} = 2mol$ [1]

2. $(1 \times 14) + (4 \times 1) + (1 \times 35.5) = 53.5g/mol$ [1]

3.
a) $\frac{183.8}{6.022 \times 10^{23}} = 3.05 \times 10^{-22}g$ [1]
(Accept $3.01 \times 10^{-22}g$)
b) $\frac{118.7}{6.022 \times 10^{23}} = 1.97 \times 10^{-22}g$ [1]
(Accept $2.00 \times 10^{-22}g$)

4. $BaCl_2 + MgSO_4 \rightarrow BaSO_4 + MgCl_2$, 5mol of $BaCl_2$ makes 5mol of $BaSO_4$, 5mol of $BaSO_4$ = $5 \times (137.3 + 32 + (4 \times 16))g/mol$ [1]; = 1166.5g [1]

The stoichiometry of the reaction is 1 : 1 ratio reactant to product.

5. B [1]

Page 36 Energetics
1.
a) Energy is taken in from the environment / surroundings [1]
b) The energy comes from Atu's leg (heat energy) [1]

2.
a) bond breaking: 436 + 243 = 679kJ/mol [1]; bond making: 2 × 431 = 862kJ/mol [1]; bond making (ΔH) = 679 – 862 = –183kJ/mol [1]; the reaction is exothermic [1]
b) A correctly drawn reaction profile for an exothermic reaction [1]

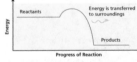

Reactants — Products — Progress of Reaction — Energy — Energy is transferred to surroundings

Pages 37–38 Practice Questions

Page 37 Types of Chemical Reactions
1. A [1]; C [1]

Remember, oxidisation is the addition of oxygen.

2. Oxidation is loss of electrons [1]; and reduction is gain of electrons [1]
3.
a) $2Na(s) + Cl_2(g) \rightarrow 2NaCl(s)$ [2]
(1 mark for correct balancing; 1 mark for correct state symbols); sodium is oxidised and chlorine is reduced [1]
b) $2Mg(s) + O_2(g) \rightarrow 2MgO(s)$ [2]
(1 mark for correct balancing; 1 mark for correct state symbols); magnesium is oxidised and oxygen is reduced [1]
c) $2Li(s) + Br_2(g) \rightarrow 2LiBr(s)$ [2] (1 mark for correct balancing; 1 mark for correct state symbols); lithium is oxidised and bromine is reduced [1]
d) $CuO(s) + H_2(g) \rightarrow Cu(s) + H_2O(l)$ [2] (1 mark for correct balancing; 1 mark for correct state symbols); copper is reduced and hydrogen is oxidised [1]

4.
a) $H^+(aq)$ [1]
b) $OH^-(aq)$ [1]
5. acid + base → salt + water [1]
6.
a) $H_2SO_4(aq) + 2NaOH(aq) \rightarrow Na_2SO_4(aq) + 2H_2O(l)$ [2]
(1 mark for correct reactants; 1 mark for correct products)
b) Na^+ [1]; SO_4^{2-} [1]
c) $H^+(aq) + OH^-(aq) \rightarrow H_2O(l)$ [2] (1 mark for correct ions; 1 mark for correct product)

Page 38 pH, Acids and Neutralisation
1. An acid that does not fully dissociate when dissolved in water [1]
2.
a) $2mol/dm^3$ H_2SO_4 [1]
b) $3mol/dm^3$ HNO_3 [1]
3. 1000 times greater (10 × 10 × 10 or 10^3) [1]

Page 38 Electrolysis
1.
a) Cations [1]
b) Anions [1]
2. The process of breaking down ionic compounds into simpler substances using an electric current [1]
3. Table salt is a solid at room temperature and pressure and electrolysis only works if the ion is in solution or molten [1]
4. Set up an electrolytic cell using a nail as the cathode [1]; and copper for the anode [1]; fill with copper(II) sulfate solution and apply an electric current [1]
5.
a) Because they do not react with the products of electrolysis or the electrolyte [1]
b) Platinum electrodes are very expensive / the same results can be achieved using cheaper electrodes [1]

Pages 39–41 Review Questions

Page 39 Types of Chemical Reactions
1. A [1]; D [1]
2.
a) Iron(III) oxide [1]
b) Carbon monoxide [1]

c) $Fe_2O_3(s) + 3CO(g) \rightarrow 2Fe(s) + 3CO_2(g)$
[2] (1 mark for correct reactants;
1 mark for correct products)
a) $2AgNO_3(aq) + Cu(s) \rightarrow$
$Cu(NO_3)_2(aq) + 2Ag(s)$ **[2]**
(1 mark for correct reactants; 1 mark
for correct products)
b) Silver **[1]**
c) Copper nitrate **[1]**
d) Silver is reduced as it gains an
electron to become solid silver **[1]**;
copper is oxidised as it loses two
electrons to become an ion **[1]**

age 40 pH, Acids and Neutralisation
a) $Mg(OH)_2(aq) + \underline{2HCl(aq)} \rightarrow$
$MgCl_2(aq) + 2H_2O(l)$ **[1]**
b) $\underline{H_2SO_4(aq)} + 2NaOH(aq) \rightarrow$
$Na_2SO_4(aq) + 2H_2O(l)$ **[1]**
c) $\underline{2CH_3COOH(aq) + 2Na(s)} \rightarrow$
$H_2(g) + 2CH_3COONa(aq)$ **[1]**
d) $\underline{2HF(aq)} + Mg(s) \rightarrow MgF_2(aq) + H_2(g)$
[1]
a) calcium + sulfuric acid $\rightarrow$ calcium
sulfate + hydrogen **[1]**
b) Above calcium **[1]**
a) $HNO_3(aq) + NaOH(aq) \rightarrow$
$NaNO_3(aq) + H_2O(l)$ **[2]**
(1 mark for correct reactants; 1 mark
for correct products)
b) $Na^+(aq)$ **[1]**; $NO_3^-(aq)$ **[1]**
c) $H^+(aq) + OH^-(aq) \rightarrow H_2O(l)$ **[2]** (1 mark
for correct ions; 1 mark for correct
product)
A strong acid dissociates completely **[1]**
10 000 ($10 \times 10 \times 10 \times 10$ or 10^4) **[1]**

age 41 Electrolysis
Molten or in solution **[1]**
a) C **[1]**
b) anion = oxygen **[1]**; cation =
hydrogen **[1]**
c) i) $2O^{2-}(aq) \rightarrow O_2(g) + 4e^-$ **[1]**
ii) $2H^+(aq) + 2e^- \rightarrow H_2(g)$ **[1]**
$X = Cu^{2+}(aq)$ **[1]**; $Y = SO_4^{2-}$ (and OH^-) **[1]**

Notes

Periodic Table

Group headers: (1) (2) (3) (4) (5) (6) (7) (0) corresponding to 1 2 ... 13 14 15 16 17 18

Key
atomic number
symbol
name
relative atomic mass

1	2	3	4	5	6	7	8	9	10	11	12	13	14	15	16	17	18
1 **H** hydrogen 1.0																	2 **He** helium 4.0
3 **Li** lithium 6.9	4 **Be** beryllium 9.0											5 **B** boron 10.8	6 **C** carbon 12.0	7 **N** nitrogen 14.0	8 **O** oxygen 16.0	9 **F** fluorine 19.0	10 **Ne** neon 20.2
11 **Na** sodium 23.0	12 **Mg** magnesium 24.3											13 **Al** aluminum 27.0	14 **Si** silicon 28.1	15 **P** phosphorus 31.0	16 **S** sulfur 32.1	17 **Cl** chlorine 35.5	18 **Ar** argon 39.9
19 **K** potassium 39.1	20 **Ca** calcium 40.1	21 **Sc** scandium 45.0	22 **Ti** titanium 47.9	23 **V** vanadium 50.9	24 **Cr** chromium 52.0	25 **Mn** manganese 54.9	26 **Fe** iron 55.8	27 **Co** cobalt 58.9	28 **Ni** nickel 58.7	29 **Cu** copper 63.5	30 **Zn** zinc 65.4	31 **Ga** gallium 69.7	32 **Ge** germanium 72.6	33 **As** arsenic 74.9	34 **Se** selenium 79.0	35 **Br** bromine 79.9	36 **Kr** krypton 83.8
37 **Rb** rubidium 85.5	38 **Sr** strontium 87.6	39 **Y** yttrium 88.9	40 **Zr** zirconium 91.2	41 **Nb** niobium 92.9	42 **Mo** molybdenum 95.9	43 **Tc** technetium	44 **Ru** ruthenium 101.1	45 **Rh** rhodium 102.9	46 **Pd** palladium 106.4	47 **Ag** silver 107.9	48 **Cd** cadmium 112.4	49 **In** indium 114.8	50 **Sn** tin 118.7	51 **Sb** antimony 121.8	52 **Te** tellurium 127.6	53 **I** iodine 126.9	54 **Xe** xenon 131.3
55 **Cs** cesium 132.9	56 **Ba** barium 137.3	57-71 lanthanides	72 **Hf** hafnium 178.5	73 **Ta** tantalum 180.9	74 **W** tungsten 183.8	75 **Re** rhenium 186.2	76 **Os** osmium 190.2	77 **Ir** iridium 192.2	78 **Pt** platinum 195.1	79 **Au** gold 197.0	80 **Hg** mercury 200.5	81 **Tl** thallium 204.4	82 **Pb** lead 207.2	83 **Bi** bismuth 209.0	84 **Po** polonium	85 **At** astatine	86 **Rn** radon
87 **Fr** francium	88 **Ra** radium	89-103 actinides	104 **Rf** rutherfordium	105 **Db** dubnium	106 **Sg** seaborgium	107 **Bh** bohrium	108 **Hs** hassium	109 **Mt** meitnerium	110 **Ds** darmstadtium	111 **Rg** roentgenium	112 **Cn** copernicium	114 **Fl** flerovium		116 **Lv** livermorium			